Spotlight on Equine Nutrition TeleSeminar Series

Easy Keeper
Making It Easy to Keep Him Healthy

Juliet M. Getty, Ph.D.

© 2013 Juliet M. Getty, Ph.D.
All Rights Reserved.

No part of this publication may be reproduced, stored in a retrieval system, or transmitted, in any form or by any means, electronic, mechanical, photocopying, recording or otherwise, without the written permission of the author.

The Easy Keeper was transcribed from a teleseminar presented by Dr. Juliet M. Getty. Transcription by Darlene J. Backer, CMT (DarleneJBacker@gmail.com). Book design, editing and publication preparation by Elizabeth Testa, Testa Creative Associates (www.TestaCreativeAssociates.com).

ISBN-13: 978-1483956800
ISBN-10: 1483956806

Printed in the United States of America

Preface & Disclaimer

Spotlight on Equine Nutrition: Easy Keeper is the transcript of a teleseminar given by Dr. Juliet M. Getty. This booklet is part of the "Spotlight on Equine Nutrition" series based on Dr. Getty's teleseminars. The goals of offering the transcript in written form are, first, to make it a useful reference resource for anyone to use, and second, to refresh the teleseminar participant's memory of materials covered. It is not necessary for the reader to have attended the teleseminar to get full value from the book.

At all times, Dr. Getty makes every effort to present the most accurate and helpful information based on her expertise and on the most reliable sources. She, her editor, transcriptionist, and publisher take no responsibility for any results or damages that might be obtained from the reliance on the information and recommendations made in this book. We further take no responsibility for the inherent risks of activities involving horses, including equine behavior changes that might result in personal injury.

Advice about nutrition, especially in the case of illness, injury, disorders, or conditions requiring medical treatment, is not intended to take the place of proper veterinary care. It may be used in conjunction with such care to facilitate healing and maintain health. The information provided by Getty Equine Nutrition, LLC is presented for the purpose of educating horse owners. Suggested feeds, supplements, and procedures are administered voluntarily with the understanding that any adverse reaction is the responsibility of the owner. Furthermore, Getty Equine Nutrition, LLC cannot be held accountable for a horse's response, whether favorable or adverse, to nutritional intervention.

This is not a verbatim transcript. Obvious comments about technical matters relevant to the teleseminar process have been omitted, along with questions and answers off the specific topic at hand. Some text editing has been done to increase reading ease and text searchability. Mention of a specific product or brand name is not intended to imply that other companies offer inferior products. Dr. Getty means no intention of trademark infringement by the omission of the ® or ™ designation; all product names mentioned are presumed trade-protected.

Juliet M. Getty, Ph.D. is an internationally respected writer and lecturer on equine nutrition. She is the Contributing Nutrition Editor for the *Horse Journal,* and her comprehensive reference book, **Feed Your Horse Like a Horse**, has educated countless horsemen and women in the science behind sound equine feeding practices. She hosts a monthly teleseminar series, one episode of which forms the basis for this adapted transcription. Her informative e-newsletter, *Forage for Thought*, is read by several thousand subscribers every month; she is also available for private consultations and speaking engagements.

The *Spotlight on Equine Nutrition Series* currently offers these teleseminar transcriptions (with more on the way):

    Aging Horse
    Deciphering Ingredients Lists
    Easy Keeper
    Feeding for Healthy Joints
    Laminitis
    Whole Foods

Dr. Getty offers a generous serving of other equine nutrition knowledge at www.GettyEquineNutrition.com.

Introduction

Equine obesity is a difficult yet highly common issue among horses all over the world, and in this teleseminar we will look at the causes, prevention and solutions. In my resource book, **Feed Your Horse Like a Horse**, I talk a great deal about weight management in Chapter 12. This teleseminar goes into far more detail than what is covered in the book, in addition to which, we will also address your questions.

Research on equine obesity actually started with studies on human obesity, looking at elements like hormonal responses and so on. Then the research moved to horses, and, lo and behold, we find that the drivers of weight issues for people are, for the most part, the same as for horses. So that gives a good idea of where we're headed in this teleseminar, and if you have any pounds to shed, then you might also find this helpful for yourself (although when we get to talking about hay, I don't think that will apply necessarily…).

First, let's look at the root causes for equine obesity.

Chapter One
Defining the Problem and Its Causes

Insulin and leptin resistance, plus inflammation

When you have an overweight horse, the horse has excess body fat, and when the amount of body fat is high, that is generally a sign of insulin resistance. This is especially true when body fat shows up in particular regions of the body, such as in a cresty neck, fat going down the spine (look for that infamous crease going down the spine), on the tailhead, certainly over the ribs, on the shoulders, even over the eyes and on the chest. Even if the ribs can be seen, sometimes we'll see fat deposits in these areas. But all overweight horses (regardless of regional fat deposits) will have some degree of insulin resistance. It is important to keep in mind that when the body fat is elevated, it causes insulin to rise, leading to insulin resistance.

Insulin resistance is the principal culprit behind such devastating conditions as laminitis. This has to do with two main issues. First, elevated insulin stimulates receptors with the hoof's laminae to grow abnormally. Second, a vicious cycle ensues when body fat is elevated: Body fat produces inflammatory molecules called cytokines that damage the hoof tissue. Cytokines disrupt insulin action, reducing the cell's insulin sensitivity. The fatter your horse becomes, the more cytokines he produces, leading to elevated insulin, leading to even more fat.

Body fat also causes another hormone, called leptin, to rise. There is fascinating research about this hormone. Leptin is secreted by the adipose (fat) tissue; it tells the brain to stop eating. Once a horse of normal weight has had enough to eat, the leptin level will rise and that will signal the horse that he's full and satisfied. Then over time, the leptin level will drop down, and as it gets lower and lower, then his appetite signal will return and he'll want to eat some more. With the overweight horse, however, this mechanism gets out of whack. With the overweight or over-fat horse, the leptin is no longer well received; in other words, the signal that the brain is supposed to get that says *I'm no longer hun-*

gry doesn't happen, so the leptin level continues to rise and rise and rise, very much like insulin resistance. Insulin is responsible for getting glucose into the cells, but if the cells are resistant to it, then glucose isn't delivered to the cells and so the insulin level keeps rising in a fruitless attempt to do its assigned job. The same thing happens with leptin. So the overweight horse is not only insulin resistant but leptin resistant.

In an effort to help the horse lose weight, more times than not the horse owner will be advised to severely restrict the amount that the horse eats, and this starts a vicious cycle: When you restrict forage and the horse stands for many hours on an empty stomach, the leptin level eventually drops as the horse loses some weight; when the leptin level drops, that signals the horse to eat more. Perhaps he'll lose some body fat, but his system—suspecting impending starvation—will keep the leptin level artificially low, and that will make him desperate to eat more; when normal feeding is resumed, he will overeat due to leptin resistance, and he will put the weight back on quickly. It's very similar in humans; a person who loses a lot of weight will very often put it back on simply because leptin now is declined, telling that person that he needs to eat more.

By restricting forage, we have created a situation where the insulin is elevated and the leptin is not being well received. Now, combine that with the fact that body fat causes inflammation. Body fat releases inflammatory molecules called cytokines, and these cytokines cause inflammation, which can damage the heart vessels, liver and kidney, as well as cause pain and—on top of all that—create more leptin resistance. Inflammation is a serious problem with the overweight horse.

What we need to do is calm all this stuff down. We need to reduce inflammation, we need to lower the blood insulin levels, and we need to reduce the body fat. It all fits together in one important effort. But how do we do that?

Four Keys

There are **four keys** to helping your horse lose weight in a way that doesn't make him gain it all back, that doesn't keep him inflamed, and that allows him to be healthy: **reduce stress, reduce calories, reduce inflammation,** and **increase exercise**.

Keep these in mind as we progress through this discussion. But first, I want to go ahead and talk about some numbers, since weight management is somewhat of a numbers game.

Chapter Two
First, Know the Numbers

Body Condition Score

The first number to know is the body condition score. You may already be familiar with the Henneke Body Condition Scoring System, which is something that we nutritionists use. (In **Feed Your Horse Like a Horse**, it's on page 173.) The horse's body is scored from 1-9: 1 is emaciated and near death, and 9 is very heavy with bulging fat all over the body. What we look for in a healthy horse, depending somewhat on the breed, is a score somewhere between a 4 and a 6. Some breeds, like Thoroughbreds for example, might score a healthy weight closer to a 4, while Hafflingers might be at their normal score at closer to a 6, but we want at least to be able *feel* the ribs. There might be some fat over the ribs, but when we press on the rib cage, there shouldn't be a great amount of regional fat accumulation. Above a body condition score of 7—regardless of breed—the horse is considered to be obese. This is the kind of overweight problem we're talking about in this teleseminar.

How Much Does My Horse Weigh?

It is useful to know how much your horse weighs. (Again referring to my book, there's a handy formula on page 168.) Certainly a scale would give you the best information, but not many barns have one. If you have a weight tape, that will give you a good estimate; you can usually pick one up at the feed store. Or simply use a conventional tape measure, and follow this procedure: Take your horse's length in inches measured in a straight line from the point of the shoulder to the buttocks. Then measure your horse's girth in inches. Next, use this formula: multiply the girth x the girth x the length, and divide that number by 330. For my international folks who will want the weight in kilograms, measure the length and girth in centimeters and follow the same formula (girth x girth x length) but instead of dividing by 330, divide by 11,900.

How Many Calories Does He Need?

It's also helpful to know approximately how many calories the horse needs to maintain a healthy weight. That's a tough one to determine exactly, but I can give you a range. It varies with the size of the horse, of course, and it varies with the activity level.

For maintenance, an adult horse that is not exercised would need between 30 and 36 kilocalories per kilogram of body weight. The formula works like this: First, convert your horse's weight to kilograms by dividing pounds by 2.2 (so an 1100 pound horse weighs 500 kgs). At 30 kilocalories/kg, that 500 kg horse would require about 15,000 kilocalories. Since in horse nutrition we use megacalories, you would divide that by 1000, which means 15,000 kilocalories is the same as 15 megacalories.

For the other extreme, the highly exercised horse, the range is somewhere between 70 and 83 kilocalories/kilogram. So, at the lower end of kilocalories, the active 500 kilogram horse would need about 35 megacalories per day.

To put this in perspective, 20 pounds of a grass hay with 0.9 megacalories per pound would give you 18 megacalories and that would fulfill the need for the maintenance horse. 35 pounds of the same hay would give you 31.5 megacalories and that would come close to meeting the need for a highly exercised horse. (If I've lost you on the numbers, feel free to email me at gettyequinenutrition@gmail.com. We'll cover getting hay analyzed in a moment.)

Cresty Neck—Is It Normal?

There is one other number I want to give you before we go into the specifics of helping your horse lose weight. How do you know if your horse's body fat level is dangerous to his health? In particular, some breeds naturally display some crestiness to the neck and that doesn't mean the horse is necessarily overweight. For the answer, remember this number: 0.63. How does that apply? If the horse's neck circumference measurement divided by his height (at the wither) equals more than 0.63, then your horse's neck is considered to display the true "cresty neck" regional fat deposit.

To measure the neck, first measure the distance from the poll to the wither, and then find the mid-point by dividing that distance in half. At the mid-point, take the circumference of the neck. For example, if the distance from the poll to the wither is 36 inches, then you would take a circumference of the horse's neck at half of 36 inches, or 18 inches, from the poll. If the circumference measurement comes out to be 42 inches and your horse is 16 hands high, or 64 inches, you would divide 42 by 64, which gives you 0.66, and that's definitely the kind of cresty neck that goes beyond a breed characteristic.

Now you have a sense of how to determine if your horse is truly overweight, and if so, by how much. Next, we'll cover some things that we can do to reduce body fat and to help your horse lose weight. Remember our four keys? Here we go.

Chapter Three
The Four Keys

True Free Choice Feeding

I am going to digress here for just a moment. I stress giving hay free choice (because, simplistically put, an empty stomach keeps the horse overweight) but if you haven't fed this way before, here are the basic tenets of free choice feeding even for the obese or overweight horse:

a. Make sure your hay is appropriately low-calorie/low NSC. NSC is the sum of simple sugars, starch and fructan. It is calculated by adding % water-soluble carbohydrates (WSC) plus % starch. It should be no higher than 12% NSC and no more than .88 Mcals/lb, on an as-sampled basis.

b. Then give your horse all the hay that he could possibly eat; in fact, give him *more* than he can possibly eat.

The key is to not ever let him run out, *not even for ten minutes*, and I don't mean just in the daytime, I mean at night, too; there has to be some hay left over in the morning.

For the first few days, even the first few weeks for some horses, they will start to eat a lot more and it will drive you nuts. But as long as you know that the hay is low in NSC, you can relax because once he gets the message that there's always hay there, that it never runs out, then, and only then, will he calm down. His instincts will kick in and he'll start to walk away from hay, and then you can breathe a sigh of relief because that's the first sign that he's starting to self-regulate.

Most horses start to adjust within about a week or two, although a few will take longer. But if you allow him to run out, even for ten minutes, then he'll never get that signal; in his mind he always will run out of hay and he'll continue to eat it very quickly and eat a lot of it. You want essentially to mimic how a horse would be in a wild situation where he moves from place to place looking for that morsel of grass and is able to do that all the time.

All the time means even at night. Horses don't sleep at night like we do. Some of you may be chuckling, but I get this comment or question quite a bit. I do find that a lot of people think that that's the case; that they don't eat very much at night, that they sleep more. That's not true. Horses will be awake most of the time. They'll nap, of course, as you know, for 15-20 minutes here and there, but that only adds up to about two or three hours total per day and it's not consecutive. So keep that hay in front of them all the time.

Now, on to the four keys.

1. Reduce stress

Reducing stress is the first step. For many readers, this will be a familiar refrain; if it's new to you, I think you'll find it fascinating. Lots of things cause your horse stress, but *one of the main causes of stress is not allowing your horse to graze.* The horse's digestive system is designed to have forage flowing through it all the time. A horse is not meant to have an empty stomach, and this makes sense if you look at the horse's physiology.

A horse's stomach produces acid constantly, unlike our own that produces acid only when we eat. A horse's stomach produces acid even when it's empty. Why? Because it's not designed to ever be empty; horses are supposed to chew all the time. Chewing produces saliva, which is a natural antacid. So if the horse has an empty stomach, that acid can cause ulcers, and then it can trickle down to the hindgut where it can damage the beneficial bacteria that live there. A change in the bacterial population can interfere with vitamin production, it can cause colic, it can cause laminitis. And an empty stomach doesn't only cause pain (a stressor in itself), it also causes mental stress because it goes against the horse's innate instincts.

This is not a small thing; when the horse is stressed, that causes the release of the stress hormone called cortisol. As cortisol rises, it causes insulin to rise and when insulin rises that causes leptin resistance as well. When we have these two things happening, that tells the body, *hey, you're in starvation mode, you had better hold onto fat,* and as we have discussed, when insulin is elevated the body will not burn fat.

The unsuccessful scenario I typically see is the well-intentioned horse owner trying to take some weight off his horse puts him in a dry lot without anything to graze on, and the horse doesn't lose weight. (And if he's suffered from laminitis in the past he could relapse because elevated insulin can also lead to laminitis—more on that in my Laminitis teleseminar.)

Back to calming all this down. If you break the stress cycle, then you cause cortisol to calm down, which causes insulin to drop, which in turn allows the horse to burn body fat. So remember that an empty stomach certainly causes stress.

There are other things often done to an overweight horse that cause stress—for example, grazing muzzles. Grazing muzzles may be beneficial for some horses if they accept them calmly, but they should be used no more than 3-4 hours per day; however, these devices can be very frustrating. If you have a horse that works all day just to get that darn thing off, or enlists the help of a buddy horse to pull it off, you're going to have a stressed horse and that's going to defeat your purpose. He will not lose weight. Slow feeders can be excellent (there are many different ones, but basically they are feeders that slow down the rate at which horses can grab hay), but they have to be introduced slowly to prevent the frustration cycle from starting up. Frustration is a form of stress, and anything that causes stress will lead to or maintain obesity.

2. Reduce calories

Know your feed. Analyze your hay. The price is generally reasonable, and it's the best money you'll ever spend. Send a sample into Equi-Analytical Labs, (www.equi-analytical.com), and order the Equi-Tech test. It gives you a lot of information.

Remember, you want your hay to be low in NSC. I like to look for hay that has less than 12% on an as-sampled basis.

But there's another thing that most people ignore, and that is the calories. The calories are listed at the top of the hay analysis report as *digestible energy*. In order for your horse to lose weight, the hay needs to be offered free choice but it also needs to be low in calories. An analogy would be this: If you wanted to lose weight and I said you could have all the chocolate cake you want all day long, anytime, 24/7, you would think I was crazy, and you would be correct, because chocolate cake is very high in calories. But if I said to you, yeah, you can eat all you want anytime you want as long as you have something low in calories—say, have all the lettuce and cucumbers you want—then that makes more sense. So what I'm saying is that your horse should have all the hay that he wants to keep his stomach filled, his digestive system working properly and his stress level down, but you can't give him chocolate cake; it's not enough just to feed free choice—we also need to make sure that the hay is low in calories.

This means you have to look at the caloric content of the hay. Ideally it should be less than 0.88 megacalories/pound which is about 1.94 megacalories/kilogram, and that is the upper limit.

Protein is one of the main factors that makes hay high in calories. Legumes such as alfalfa tend to be higher in calories because they're higher in protein. The NSC of alfalfa is often much lower than grass hay such as timothy or orchard grass, and yet it has more calories because of the higher amount of protein. This is why I don't recommend feeding alfalfa free choice. Give your horse free choice of a good grass hay that is low in calories and certainly low in NSC.

What about pasture?

Now a word about pasture and the overweight horse. Depending on the time of year, depending on the time of day, depending on the temperature, pasture can be very high in NSC, so it is not generally the best choice for helping a horse to lose weight. Even grass that appears dormant may have actively growing roots and tiny shoots which are high in NSC. In the spring, the fresh sprouts—so tasty to horses—are full of sugars and starch as well. This is not the appropriate diet for an insulin-resistant horse. Once you get your horse's weight down, however, then you can allow your horse to graze a little bit on pasture, but you have to be careful and you have to start out slow.

Here's a brief rundown on the cycle of grass growth and how it affects the NSC content:

When grass is exposed to sunlight all day, through the process of photosynthesis, it produces sugar and starch and fructan. And during the nighttime hours when there's no sunlight, then the grass burns those elements to help it grow. So the grass is at its lowest level of NSC before dawn, and then the process starts all over.

The NSC level tends to be lowest before dawn, but *only when the nighttime temperatures are warm*. If the nighttime temperatures drop below around 40 degrees Fahrenheit, then the sugar, fructan and starch remain in the grass and the grass doesn't use them to grow, so they are still high in the morning.

We typically see this in the spring when there are sunny days and at night it gets quite cold; under these conditions, the grass is higher in sugar basically all day and all night long because it just doesn't relinquish it and then continues to produce more during photosynthesis. We see it again in the fall. So, when it starts to get cold at night and the daytime is sunny, you have to be aware that the grass may be too high in sugar. However, if it's a cloudy day and especially if it's a warm cloudy day, the grass will be lower in sugar, fructan and starch.

But one more important thing to keep in mind: Anything that stresses grass, whether it be cold temperatures, whether it be drought, whether it be overgrazing, whether it be a lot of competitive weeds, whether it be a lot of sunlight, all these stressors will increase the amount of NSC in the grass.

3. Reduce inflammation

As we've seen, reducing inflammation is a critical component of weight management. The most basic thing to grasp is that *antioxidants reduce inflammation*. (See Appendix B.) Antioxidants include such things as vitamin E, vitamin C, and beta carotene (which is found in plants and which horses use to make vitamin A). These vitamins are not found in hay. They are found in fresh healthy grass, but once the grass is cut and dried and stored to make hay, the hay is dead, and it starts to lose those antioxidants which are destroyed by oxygen during and after the curing (drying) process. Therefore a hay diet needs to be supplemented with antioxidants. There are a number of commercial supplements that include those antioxidant ingredients.

Omega-3 fatty acids also reduce inflammation and ground flaxseeds are among the best sources of omega-3s; other supplements include it as well.

Supplements such as magnesium, chromium, and psyllium are also helpful. For magnesium, I suggest offering 5000 mg/250 pounds of body weight, and for chromium between 1-2 mg/250 pounds of body weight.

As for psyllium, this is a relatively new kid on the block. A very interesting study was published recently demonstrating how psyllium lowers circulating glucose, which lowers circulating insulin. We usually think of using psyllium husks in terms of sand colic, with psyllium provided seven days out of the month as a preventive. In cases of insulin resistance, it's best to give your horse about a third of a cup of psyllium per meal, which, for my international readers, is approximately 70 ml per meal, and that's every day. (By "meal" I mean a feeding that is in addition to the normal hay and/or pasture you're providing.)

Foods to avoid

Avoid foods with more omega-6 fatty acids than omega-3s because omega-6s actually increase inflammation; oils that are high in omega-6s are soybean, vegetable, corn, and hemp seed oil. And avoid iron; too much iron increases insulin resistance. Many supplements contain iron, yet forage is typically quite high in it, so the horse is already getting enough. Avoid sweet feeds, too. In fact, avoid feeding anything that contains cereal grains like oats or corn or barley; these are starchy feeds, and starch and sugars (molasses is a classic example) become digested down to glucose and when glucose gets into the bloodstream, it causes insulin to rise–and now you know the rest of the process: When insulin goes up, body fat goes up as well.

4. Exercise

The final element to include in weight management is movement. Exercise. Exercise does three things. We all know that exercise burns calories and that's great, but exercise also builds muscle, and whenever you build muscle, you increase the metabolic rate, which is the rate at which your horse burns calories when he's at rest. Muscle is more metabolically active than fat and so the more muscle mass your horse has, the faster he or she will burn calories. And finally, exercise causes the body cells to become more sensitive (less resistant) to insulin and to leptin. With exercise, then, insulin resistance and leptin resistance start to decline, allowing your horse to burn body fat and to not have a voracious appetite anymore. It's a critical component to solving the obesity problem.

In fact, movement in general is very helpful just to keep the digestive tract functioning, because it's made of muscles and it must move. A horse that stands in a stall for hours and hours and hours will often colic just because the intestines become flabby and can twist and turn and telescope (intussuscept).

It need not be arduous exercise. Just give the horse opportunities to move, the way he was designed to do.

Chapter Four
Questions & Answers

Weight control for ponies: Kay has a 21-year-old Icelandic gelding. She doesn't ride him and so it's difficult for her to exercise him. She has a track paddock, about two acres, and then she has 40 acres with a lot of grass as well as blackberries. She is worried that he may develop laminitis.

> *Answer:* Icelandics are interesting because we call them horses but metabolically, they're actually ponies, and all ponies are genetically insulin resistant so we have to really watch out for their sugar and starch intake. They should not have a lot of fat either. So, Kay, you have very valid concerns. I would suggest, since you're not aware of what's in the grass in your 40 acre area, that you analyze it. Sometimes you may be surprised to find the pasture has lower NSC than your grass hay. And since I do encourage movement, the larger the space the better. Then, when the grass is dormant in winter, put hay out, a low-sugar, low-starch hay. Put it out in several places to encourage movement. Don't let him stand in one place and just eat and eat and eat. One thing to note: Blackberries are great tasting, but they're just too high in sugar for your horse, so watch that depending on the season.
>
> One other thing I want to mention to you, Kay. This isn't related to obesity but your horse's age: Make sure he is getting some vitamin C since he's no longer producing enough of it at his age.

Reviewing a feeding program holistically. Lisa has several different horses but one is overweight and one is a mini. She wants to know what I think of her feeding program.

> *Answer:* Lisa's horses are on grass, and as I mentioned earlier, grass may not be the best thing for the overweight horse because it does tend to be higher in sugars and starch at certain times of the year. Minis are genetically predisposed toward insulin resistance as well. You're feeding Buckeye Grow 'N Win. I don't think that this is necessary; it is 30% protein and that's not appropriate for an adult horse or for a mini. I would give

that level of protein only to a growing horse, one that's recovering from an injury or surgery, or a pregnant mare. The timothy pellets as you're feeding them are very nice. About the probiotic: If you're going to feed a probiotic, make sure that it has billions of CFUs. Probios has a low amount of colony forming units (CFUs); it has millions and that's not enough--it's not even enough for you. The oats you're feeding are not appropriate; no oats, no cereal grains at all for the overweight horse and certainly not for a mini. You asked me about a supplement called Cur-Ost, which I took a look at. It contains curcumin, as well as other antioxidants. Curcumin itself is an anti-inflammatory, which is good. We want to reduce inflammation.

Chelated minerals. Lisa also asked if trace minerals need to be chelated to be absorbed.

Answer: Chelated minerals are connected to another substance (usually amino acids). They do have a slightly better bioavailability than inorganic versions; however, it's not significant enough to avoid inorganic versions altogether... Minerals can be bitter, however, and inorganic is sometimes more palatable to very picky eaters since chelation seems to increase bitterness.

Breed propensities and insulin resistance. Jeannie wants to know if I think certain breeds have a propensity to become easy keepers; in particular she asks about Rocky Mountain Horses.

Answer: Genetics play a major role in body composition, metabolic rate, and hormonal balance, all of which affect the way horses process food. Most horses can develop insulin resistance (even Thoroughbreds, though it's not as common). But certain breeds, including Quarter Horses, Arabians, Morgans, Tennessee Walkers, saddlebreds, all the draft breeds, minis, ponies, donkeys and mules, have a more pronounced genetic propensity for insulin resistance so you have to be vigilant about keeping their body weight at a normal level. I have not found a consistent pattern of insulin resistance in Rockies.

High protein, low NSC—safe to feed a horse with a history of laminitis? Christine has a draft-Quarter Horse cross that has had laminitis. Her new hay tested as low in starch and sugar as the timothy grass that she was using before but the protein level was 15%; should she feed something high in protein even though it is low in NSC?

Answer: As mentioned above, Quarter Horses and draft breeds are genetically predisposed toward insulin resistance and becoming easy keepers. The high protein level in the hay adds calories, so that can cause weight gain. I would watch this carefully.

Soy and hoof pain. Christina also fed something soy-based that caused her horse's foot to become sore. She asks the reason for that.

Answer: Some horses are sensitive to soy-based products. Soy is a legume. Alfalfa is a legume. And I like alfalfa and I like soy most of the time because they both boost the overall protein quality, allowing the horse to have all the amino acids or building blocks he needs to repair tissue, to build new tissue, to build antibodies, hormones, enzymes, and the like. But legumes do contain plant forms of estrogen and though it's not proven, I have some suspicion that phytoestrogens or plant estrogens may cause some problems with the feet.

Flaxseed meal. Christina feeds Omega Horse Shine for flaxseed meal. Is this appropriate?

Answer: Omega Horse Shine contains oats, which is a cereal grain and that is not appropriate for an overweight horse. By the way, it's not appropriate for a horse that's prone toward ulcers either, so for a Thoroughbred, especially one that is off the track, feeding oats would not be a good thing either. The flaxseed meal that I recommend is called "Nutra-Flax." It is just plain ground flaxseed that's stabilized and has a small amount of calcium added to correct for the high phosphorus levels in flax. (It's made by Horse Tech. You can look at the Horse Tech website; I also carry it through my website.) You also wanted to know, Christina, if you should add magnesium to the diet for an insulin resistant horse. Absolutely.

For hoof supplementation, since hay has nutritional gaps, I would suggest a flaxseed meal-based vitamin and mineral supplement. My favorite is called Glanzen Lite Complete, and the complete part is the very important thing. It has all the vitamins and minerals a horse needs plus the hoof preparation, so you don't need an additional hoof supplement. It's a custom-made product made by Horse Tech; you can purchase it through my website or Horse Tech can get it for you as well. My goal is not to sell you supplements; it's to give you some suggestions, but I have been recommending that one for a long time just because it's so appropriate.

Situations that prevent free choice feeding. Karen's insulin resistant easy keeper is turned out 24/7 on a dry lot with two other geldings that are not insulin resistant. The horses compete with one another. If she feeds a lower quality hay free choice, the thinner ones lose weight but the easy keeper continues to gain weight even though she is using hay nets. Karen wonders if there ever is a situation where horses simply cannot be fed free choice.

Answer: The stress of competing for food, even the stress of dealing with potentially grumpy, hungry, thin paddock companions, could increase the tendency to gain weight in the easy keeper. I would suggest that you try to reduce the stress as much as possible. Then, as I mentioned, the hay has to be low in calories, so it's best to have it analyzed to make sure that that's the case because the NSC, for example, can be low but the calories may still be too high if it contains a legume (such as alfalfa) driving up the protein. So check that out first and then put hay in as many places as possible, encouraging your horse to seek out where the next pile might be so that she's not standing in one place. This will also help her avoid harassment from the others. We also need to make sure that she's getting the supplements I mentioned. Magnesium and chromium are best supplied by a supplement called Quiessence (Foxden Equine). And include psyllium pellets at one-third of a cup per meal.

Free choice feeding and behavior. Wendy offers a comment, rather than a question. She says that before they had free choice hay, her horses were poorly behaved, with bad habits such as biting the stall walls and chewing other wood.

Response: This makes sense when you remember that horses' stomachs continuously produce acid, which is meant to be neutralized by saliva created by chewing. Horses with empty stomachs will chew on whatever they can get their teeth on—wood or walls or fence posts. They'll eat their own manure. Sometimes they'll drool. Anything to produce saliva. And they get very grumpy. But once you start feeding them free choice, not only will their weight stabilize, but their behavior will change as well. It's remarkable. You won't notice them grabbing at the hay when you bring it out to them; they'll just be calm. So many things will improve: They'll be easier to train, they'll be easier under saddle. They will just be much better horses because they're not in pain anymore.

Feeding the stabled horse which has to compete for food. Diane has a Welsh pony which is stabled with other horses. At the stable, the horses are fed three times a day and they eat every speck of hay. She has found that if she puts in a natural feeder, her pony's stablemate will dominate and keep her pony from eating. The other horse owner doesn't want her horse fed free choice because she fears weight gain. So Diane wants to know what I recommend for those who board and don't have control over feeding.

Answer: I know this is a real problem, Diane, that a lot of folks face. Most barn managers that I've encountered don't have a good understanding of the way a horse is made. I strongly suggest, if you have my book, lend it to your barn manager or lend it to the owner of the horse that is concerned about her horse being fat and doesn't want to free choice feed. Suggest they look at my website, too. And put three hay nets out there so that the two animals can move from one to the other and have free access to hay without danger of stressful bullying. If the stablemate's owner can't be convinced, then perhaps it's time to look for another boarding situation. I know that's a harsh way of putting it, but it's your horse and you want the best for him. He depends on you.

Glanzen Lite. Diane asks what I think of this product.

Answer: Go with the Glanzen Lite Complete because the Glanzen Lite doesn't have the vitamins that are lost from hay.

NSC in soaked beet pulp and in treats. Christine wants to know the NSC of soaked beet pulp; she also asks about giving dry macaroni as a treat.

Answer: Soaking doesn't change the NSC (unless you pour off the water after you soak it), but beet pulp in general is very low in NSC, about 12%. I love beet pulp for the insulin-resistant horse because it does not raise the blood insulin levels. I couldn't help but chuckle over your question about using dry macaroni for a treat. I think you know the answer to that. Macaroni is made from wheat and wheat is a grain and the NSC is probably around 60-70 %, so that does not make is a good treat. Carrots and apples are also not a good idea. Alfalfa pellets are generally a good treat; however, you mentioned that the alfalfa pellets you found have about 31% NSC; that sounds crazy. Alfalfa is very low in sugar so there must be something else in those pellets. There may be some grain in them, so look for plain alfalfa pellets. Timothy pellets are great. For low-starch, low-sugar treats, alfalfa cubes also work nicely broken up into pieces. Then there are Skode's Horse Treats; those are fun for special occasions.

Changing food around arbitrarily. Nancy has mustangs which are easy keepers in the Colorado Rockies. They have no shelter but they have lots of trees; they get very limited formal exercise. As sort of a comfort food in the evenings, she gives them a couple of handfuls of grain which she mixes with whatever she happens to have. She wants to know if that's okay.

Answer: Ideally, Nancy, that's not okay. Feeding consistency is so important. Whenever you change a feed, you need to do it gradually to allow the bacteria that live in the hindgut to adjust, but when you change things every week or so those bacteria don't adjust. By doing this, you're increasing the risk, and it's significant, of your horse developing colic. So I don't recommend that. Furthermore, most of as the grains you mentioned are sweet feeds or contain oats; those are poison for an overweight horse, so I would not do that.

Watch Feed Labels. Nancy also asks about the original Nutrena Safe Choice, which gives me the opportunity to talk about feed labels. While the name, Safe Choice, would seem to promise this feed would be helpful for the insulin-resistant or overweight horse, its label reveals that, in fact, it is not. With an NSC of about 25%, Safe Choice is lower in starch than, for example, a sweet feed that's made from oats, which might have an NSC level of 50%, but that's still not low enough. Nutrena now offers a Special Care with 15% NSC (considerably lower, but not low enough). Purina Equine Senior, I believe, also has an NSC of about 15%. A truly safe low-starch feed will have an NSC level of less than 13%. Other senior feeds are generally lower but not all of them. Triple Crown Senior is about 12%.

When to check insulin and thyroid levels. Cindy has a 22-year-old Percheron gelding; she knows this breed is genetically predisposed to insulin resistance, and he has arthritis. She says he's a stout fellow; he's not really overweight but he does have a round belly type and she gives him orchard and Bermuda grass, all he can eat. He is a rather picky eater. Cindy wants to know how often or what month would be a good time to check his insulin and thyroid levels.

Answer: First of all, true hypothyroidism is extremely rare in horses. Testing a horse's thyroid level is not going to tell you much because various factors influence the test results; for example, the thyroid level will be low if insulin is somewhat high. Pain can also cause thyroid levels to decline. Insulin levels vary a lot as well. Stress, as we've discussed, raises insulin; in some horses, as soon as they see the vet's truck pull up, their insulin level goes up, so I don't think testing insulin is necessarily a helpful test to do, either. You can usually look at a horse and tell if he's insulin resistant. Look for the telltale fat deposits. Measure the neck circumference to the height ratio; if it's over 0.63 then you have a cresty neck.

Cindy is hoping not to have to restrict her Percheron from grazing when the grass grows as well. If you can get his weight down, then he can graze. Encourage movement, add magnesium and chromium (Quiessence is a really good idea), add psyllium, reduce inflammation by giving him omega 3s from flaxseed meal—do all these things to help him lose weight. He may not be able to graze at the most dangerous times, but perhaps you might be able to allow it for a half-hour to an hour in the morning. Around 10 to 11 am, remove him from pasture and put him in a dry lot with free-choice hay. The longer the grass is exposed to sunlight, the more sugars/starch it will produce. So by the late afternoon, the grass contains the highest amounts of NSC and therefore, should be avoided.

Thyroxine supplementation. Christina has a 6-year-old Paso Fino gelding with regional fat deposits, including a cresty neck. He eats grass hay year around out of slow-feeding nets. He gets magnesium oxide. Should he be given thyroxine supplementation?

Answer: A lot of vets will do this to help a horse lose weight. I think that it is not the best way to go. Certainly if it's used short term, for three or four months tops, it can be helpful for some horses. Thyroxine does increase the metabolic rate to some extent but it's not a magic pill. It essentially tells the thyroid gland that it's not necessary anymore, and so, after short term use, you must wean the horse off of it, because otherwise the horse's own thyroid gland will cease to function and the horse will need the supplement for the rest of his life. So I don't think this is the best solution, and I do think that it's given when it doesn't need to be. In most cases, the thyroid gland works just fine. As I mentioned, a true hypothyroid horse is very rare, and the benefits of supplementing for weight loss are short-lived.

Psyllium. Ella has a question about psyllium. In her case she had her mare on thyroxine and it had absolutely no effect after three months. Quiessence, however, did help reduce the mare's cresty neck. She wants to know if she adds psyllium, will it help her horse process forage.

Answer: Psyllium won't help process forage, Ella, but it will help lower her insulin levels (when given with each meal) and if you do have sandy soils it certainly will help with preventing sand colic to some extent. (The truly best way to prevent sand colic is to feed hay free choice, encourage movement, and provide lots of water.) Ella mentioned that the mare gets grass pasture in the afternoon and seven pounds of hay, and she is stalled overnight. I remind you to be sure there's hay left over in the morning, Ella. I don't know if seven pounds will last all through the night. A note about Quiessence: Keep in mind that with Quiessence, which is a magnesium/chromium preparation, you've got to be patient. It's going to take months before you start to see some improvement.

Psyllium safety for an HYPP gelding. Ella also asks about psyllium being safe for an HYPP gelding.

Answer: HYPP is hyperkalemic periodic paralysis, which is a genetic disorder involving abnormal potassium movement between the blood and the cells where sodium leaks into the cells, forcing potassium into the blood. Psyllium is fine. The goal is for the diet to have less than 1.5% potassium. Unsweetened psyllium has less than 1% potassium so it's very low.

PSSM and carbohydrates. Linda has an easy keeper with a history of stomach ulcers; the mare is also overweight and has PSSM (polysaccharide storage myopathy). Linda wants to know how she can keep weight off, yet still protect her against her ulcer tendency and "serve the high-fat needs" of the PSSM horse.

Answer: PSSM is another carbohydrate disorder, with diet requirements similar to those for the insulin-resistant horse but with a different mechanism at work. These horses don't actually require high fat; it's just that they can't have carbohydrates to any large extent for energy, so if you have a horse that's active and needs more calories, then you have to supply those calories from fat. But if the horse is already overweight, then you don't need to give fat. I recommend some flaxseed meal, which is high in fat but it's high in omega 3s, which is very important—you don't have to feed a large amount of it.

Remember, you protect against ulcers by providing hay free choice so that the stomach acid is always neutralized by chewing. Since your circumstances prevent your testing the horse's hay, I suggest you soak it if you can. Soak the hay for 30 minutes and then allow the mare to have that; discard the soaking water—don't give it to the mare. Avoid legumes in large quantity; you can give a small amount, maybe 10% of the total hay ration, but feed mostly free choice low-sugar, low starch hay to reduce weight. It will also reduce the chance of ulcers and it will provide her the low carbohydrate diet dictated by the PSSM.

Raw vegetable diet for forage and deworming. Karen feeds a raw veggie diet. Is it sufficient and appropriate for her horse? She believes it helps deworm.

Answer: Of course, hay is raw veggies but Karen feeds lots of things like olive oil, soaked seeds, fresh raw fruits, ground flax, apples, pears, and so on, as well as pumpkin seeds and nuts to help deworm. I don't know about deworming with those things; I would still test, Karen. Take a manure sample in every couple of months to make sure the worm count is not too high, and then you do have to paste worm with praziquantel at least once a year for tapeworms because that won't show up on a manure test, and encysted larvae as well needs to be treated. But back to the feeding question: I think that those foods are fine as long as your horse isn't overweight. I would not give apples and pears to an overweight horse; those are just too high in sugar. And do make sure that she's getting all the forage, all the hay that she wants. You couldn't possibly feed enough of these feeds to give your horse the 2-3.5% of her body weight she needs in forage; that would be a lot of fresh fruits and vegetables.

Beet pulp calories. Charlotte's trainer had her take away the free-choice orchard hay she was feeding her horse and cut back on the beet pulp. Charlotte wonders about the wisdom of this.

Answer: Beet pulp does have calories; it has about the same number of calories as oats but it doesn't create any of the insulin response. You could take away the beet pulp, you could take away concentrates of any kind, but don't ever take away forage. So have your hay analyzed, and as I mentioned, add magnesium, chromium, and psyllium, and encourage movement. If she's a youngster and likes to play, encourage toys. Put hay as far away as possible to encourage her to not stand in one place.

Allen and Page Fast Fibre. Hannah from the UK uses a feed that is called Allen and Page Fast Fibre. She wants to know what I think of it.

Answer: I think this product is fine. It's a hay replacer, usually given to horses that don't have teeth. It's high in fiber, the NSC is only 7.5%, and it's low in calories, so I see no problem using this, although ideally it's better to have hay available if a horse can chew it.

Timothy hay for ponies. Mary asks if timothy hay is okay for ponies.

Answer: Yes, absolutely, Mary, it's excellent. Not only do you want to watch the sugar and starch intake because ponies are insulin resistant, but you also want to watch the fat intake. To supplement the hay for omega-3s, you can give ponies some flaxseed meal, but not too much. Usually I recommend a half cup of flaxseed meal per 400 pounds of body weight for a *horse*. For a *pony* I would go with half of that.

Encouraging others to follow wise weight loss practices for their horses. Miriam wants to know how to encourage weight loss for her clients' horses. Her own horses live in the woods where they have access to open space; they receive hay year round and they keep their weight just fine. But she has clients that will build a dry lot and then not allow free choice; they use grazing muzzles and they restrict their horses in a small space. What can she do about this?

Answer: Miriam herself does everything right. So when you tell them about the right way, Miriam, eventually they'll get it. Many folks are reluctant to feed free choice, and it's a tough hurdle to get over, but if they learn to allow horses to be more like what they're designed to be, to be horses, then the horses will regulate their body weight, they will self-regulate their intake and eat only what their bodies need. It's only when they're deprived that they tend to eat an enormous amount. So continue to keep up the good work by encouraging them.

Platinum Performance. Jan asks what I think about Platinum Performance, and if there is something I like better. She gives her horse a scoop of Platinum Performance and a scoop of Platinum CJ.

Answer: Platinum Performance is flaxseed meal based. It's a good supplement. It's very expensive. It has a lot of things in it which are okay, a lot of amino acids, for example, but it does contain molasses (and iron), so it would not be appropriate for the insulin resistant horse. The CJ is the same thing as the Platinum Performance except it has a joint preparation in it.

I actually prefer a product called ReitSport HA-100 Lite Complete. It's flaxseed meal based and is comparable to Platinum Performance. It's not as expensive and it does have the joint preparation as well as all the necessary vitamins and minerals without the molasses and without iron.

Feeding a BLM mustang, including oats. Irene has a 3-year-old mustang that she adopted from the BLM; she feeds her horse timothy hay unrestricted and a little bit of alfalfa. She also gives crimped oats and wheat bran. She asks what I think of this program.

Answer: For a young horse in healthy weight, such as yours, I would increase your alfalfa to about 30% of the total hay ration—that's two flakes of grass hay to every one flake of alfalfa. Alfalfa boosts the protein quality.

For the overweight horse, I still like to include a little bit of alfalfa but it has to be significantly less, because it's too high in calories. It can never be offered free choice. Usually alfalfa is given sort of as a side dish. You know, you have grass hay free choice and then you offer alfalfa, no matter what the amount, kind of as a condiment on the side.

At three years, she's still growing, so avoid the grains. Seriously. As long as she is not overweight, you can give a little bit, but too much starch for young horses can lead to osteopathic disorders. I would not give her more than a pound a day.

For the record, heavy use of oats harkens back to the days before the automobile, when horses were used for transportation and needed more calories than hay could provide. So we started feeding them oats, but for the average horse today that is not appropriate. Even for horses that are heavily exercised, we need to limit them, too, because too much grain can increase acid production, and that can lead to ulcers. So, in general, high-starch diets are just not good for most horses.

Wheat bran is too high in phosphorous—I'm just not too crazy about it. It also irritates the gastrointestinal lining. So I would suggest that you fill in the gaps with either Glanzen Lite Complete or you might go with High Point for grass diets plus some Nutra-Flax.

Diatomaceous earth. Irene says she uses diatomaceous earth for deworming.

Comment: The effectiveness and safety of diatomaceous earth for this use is not proven; even if they kill the larvae, the little exoskeletons may be harming the delicate lining of the small intestine, so I'm not in favor of using it. I'd much rather you just test his manure every couple of months and then deworm as needed.

Pasture to stable transition. Wendy has two horses. In the summertime they're out 24/7, in the wintertime they're out during the day and stabled at night. Wendy is concerned about transitioning them from being stabled overnight to the spring pasture, from hay to the higher sugar and starch of the pasture grass. She doesn't have any kind of dry lot.

Answer: As you get into spring, that is a real concern if your horses are overweight. The best option would be to dry lot them with hay, but since you cannot do that, then you need to do all of the other things we've talked about, and be sure to give your horses lots and lots of walking every day to counteract the elevated insulin levels from the sugars and starches that are in the spring grasses. Riding them would make a significant difference.

Unsoaked beet pulp. Wendy also asks if it's okay to feed unsoaked beet pulp.

Answer: If you use the shredded kind, you don't need to soak it, but it is very dry so I like to soak it anyway. Feed it at ground level and ideally add some water to it; that would be the best thing to do, but it can be fed dry as long as it's not the pelleted version.

"Typical" overweight Quarter Horse. Caller has an overweight "typical" Quarter Horse that gets grass hay. She understands the recommendation to add Quiessence and the Glanzen Lite Complete, but wonders if that is all that's needed. And what should she use as a carrier?

Answer: I would go with either some alfalfa or timothy pellets, or even a small amount of unsweetened beet pulp. Beet pulp is sometimes hard to find without sugar so if you must use the kind with sugar, you can remove most of the sugar by adding some water to it and letting it sit for a few minutes and then pouring the water off. But you don't need more than a cup or so of that to carry those supplements.

To clarify: Glanzen Lite Complete is Nutra-Flax plus vitamins and minerals so it's already flaxseed meal based. Nutra-Flax is just plain ground flaxseed. So the Glanzen Lite Complete fills in the gaps that exist with hay. That's why I recommend it. But if you have another vitamin/mineral supplement that you like instead, you could feed Nutra-Flax plus that vitamin/mineral supplement.

Stress from injury and pain. Barbara asks Dr. Getty to remind everyone about how stress can also come from pain as was the case with her mare, from injury.

Response: Oh, absolutely. Any type of stress, whether it be physical (from pain or discomfort), or from being mentally challenged (such as the loss of a buddy, traveling to unfamiliar locations, a new living arrangement, etc.) can cause a hormonal change.

Psyllium mixed with beet pulp. Caller asks if she should mix psyllium with beet pulp or just lay it on top of the pulp, dry.

Answer: You can mix psyllium with anything. Usually it comes in pellets or in a powder form. The pellets some horses will simply eat right out of your hand but oftentimes it's just not palatable enough to do that, so you can mix psyllium with anything else that you're feeding.

Adding flavorings for palatability. Kris has two horses with entirely different metabolisms, sharing the same paddock. One is an older Thoroughbred that gets a nice-smelling senior feed and the other is a draft-cross with insulin resistance that gets Ontario Dehy Timothy Balance Cubes. The draft-cross is starting to get more interested in the Thoroughbred's feed than in her own. Kris is wondering if it's safe to use the flavorings that are offered on Dr. Getty's website to make the cubes more attractive to the draft-cross.

> *Answer:* You're referring to Aperti (Horsetech). These are flavored oils, and you don't use much, only about a teaspoon. So it's not going to add a significant amount of calories and it does add flavoring. That's one way to go. But, frankly, you might just go to your grocery store and pick up some banana extract. Banana is one of the favorite flavors for horses and you can just add a drop or two mixed in with some water. You might find your horses like that just as well. Apple cider vinegar is also good tasting for a lot of horses. So you can experiment with these different things. Aperti is an option, but there are other tricks out there, too.

MedVet Pharmaceuticals. Nancy asks what Dr. Getty thinks of MedVet Pharmaceutical supplements in general. She is trying to figure out a complete supplementation program for her "fat little pony." He gets mostly grass hay, occasionally a grass/alfalfa mix, and is periodically in pasture in the summer.

> *Answer:* I offer quite a few of their products through my website. I don't have everything of theirs, just some products that I think are worthwhile. For your pony, MedVet Pharmaceuticals makes products called Mega-Mag and Mega-Cell; Mega-Cell probably would be more appropriate—that's for grass diets, and it has a relatively high level of magnesium. But I like even better their product called Carb-X, which they make for insulin-resistant horses.
>
> I usually recommend Quiessence. It's a magnesium/chromium preparation. But for really stubborn cases, such as for your pony, then I move up to Carb-X. It's considerably more expensive, which is why I don't often suggest it except for stubborn cases. It has an herb called *gymnema sylvestre*, which has been used with human diabetic patients very successfully. So, I would go with Carb-X along with a small amount of flaxseed meal. That would be very helpful. You can actually add that to a vitamin/ mineral supplement because the Carb-X is not a complete vitamin/mineral

preparation. Take a look at High Point, that's made by Horse Tech. You could do High Point and Carb-X and a little bit of Nutra-Flax, or you could do Glanzen Lite Complete and some Carb-X. That would also work.

Adjusting from severe weight loss. Nancy also mentions that her pony went elsewhere for a while. When he left, he was a little on the plump side; when he came back he was a 2 or a 3 on the Henneke scale. Now, he's a 7.

Response: That's a great example of the leptin problem I mentioned earlier. When you reduce body fat and restrict diet so severely, it causes the leptin levels to decline so much that the horse never gets the signal that he needs to stop eating. So now, exercise him. Reduce stress. That's the only way you're going to get the hormonal balance back into shape.

Soaking beet pulp. Caller asks about soaking beet pulp to reduce sugar so she can feed it to her "two chubby horses."

Answer: Soak it only as long as it is necessary to plump it up. In fact, if you use warm water, it's virtually ready within two minutes. If it's cold water, then soak for about 30 minutes, but the longer you soak it, the more bacterial growth it has. You wouldn't eat something that's sitting out for two hours, or you shouldn't. The pellets do take longer to soften. If you can use hot water, that would shorten your soaking time considerably.

The sugar that is added to the beet pulp is the problem for the overweight horse. It doesn't have as many calories as fat would, but it does create the insulin response, which is what you want to diminish. So in that case, it's best to soak the beet pulp and drain the water off. If it's unsweetened, and the pellets usually are unsweetened, then you don't need to drain the water.

Knowing hay's content when analyzing isn't possible. Caller buys hay by the bale, from the same provider, but quality varies between batches, and she wonders how to make sure this is safe to feed free choice. She also asks for a recommendation between orchard and Bermuda grass, and mentions that the barn where the horse boards feeds only alfalfa.

Answer: This is a tough situation. If you can soak the hay, that would be beneficial simply to remove any excess sugars that might be in it. To soak it, you put the hay in a hay net and lower it in a water trough and let it sit for 30 minutes. Using the hay net makes it easier and less messy than simply putting the hay loose in a bucket of water.

Bermuda is lower in sugar and starch than orchard is typically; not always, but typically it is. So I would go with Bermuda. Regarding the alfalfa hay you're feeding, be very careful not to feed more than a couple of pounds a day.

Incidentally, I commend you for your effort on this challenge. I know it must be difficult, but the more you do, the better off your horses will be and then other people will see that, and then you'll help other people get back on track as well.

Brewer's Yeast. Nancy asks if Brewer's Yeast is safe for horses. She finds it listed as an ingredient on a "bug control" supplement.

Answer: Brewer's yeast is high in all the B vitamins but it's a particularly good source of vitamin B1, thiamine, which does seem to have some propensity toward repelling insects. It's not scientific; it's more anecdotal evidence, but there's no harm in giving brewer's yeast. It is safe for a fat horse.

Conclusion

I hope that you go away with at least one new piece of information tonight or that I've given you some things to think about. And keep me posted on how you're doing. Obesity is a very difficult problem for so many horses, and a challenge for their owners. Weight management does take time, it does take patience, but it does work. I've literally seen this thousands of times over the years and that's why what I propose is actually nothing new; I suppose it's so old that it's new, but it's just allowing horses to be who they are by feeding them the way they were designed to eat.

Appendix A
What It Means to Feed Free Choice

The horse's digestive tract is designed to have forage flowing through it every minute of every day. At night, too!

The intestines are made of muscles and require forage to keep them exercised and conditioned, in order to assure efficient nutrient processing and prevent colic. Furthermore, the horse's stomach continuously secretes acid, even when empty; horses need to chew to produce saliva, a natural antacid. Running out of hay is physically painful and mentally stressful, virtually assuring the formation of an ulcer. But that's not all – the hormonal response created by forage restriction tells the horse to hold on to body fat, creating a weight management nightmare and making it very difficult for the overweight horse to lose weight.

The solution: Feed your horse the way he was designed to eat.

> Step 1: *Know what you are feeding.* Test your hay and/or pasture. Especially when feeding overweight horses, the forage should be low in non-structural carbohydrates (NSC)—NSC should be less than 12% on an as-sampled basis. And it should be low in calories (known as digestible energy) at no more than 0.88 Mcals/lb on an as-sampled basis.
>
> Step 2: Once you have determined the forage is appropriate to feed, **feed it free choice**. Always have forage available, 24/7. The hay should never run out, not even for 10 minutes. And not just during the day—nighttime is important, too.

Then be patient, step back and watch your horse do what comes naturally.

Give the process approximately 2-3 weeks; most horses take less time, some take up to a month. At first he will overeat, but once he gets the message that the hay is always there, he will walk away – that's the magic moment! He will calm down, eat more slowly, and self-regulate his intake, eating only what his body needs to maintain condition.

Allow your horse to tell you how much he needs. He may even eat less than before because running out of hay is no longer an issue. Trust this will happen. Soon, your horse's weight will adjust into the normal, healthy range, his behavior will be more natural and steady, and his health will be more vibrant.

Appendix B
Antioxidants—The Unsung Heroes

Antioxidant. The word implies that it *goes against* something involving oxygen. But oxygen is necessary for life, so why need something contrary to it? The truth is that oxidation of carbohydrates, proteins, and fats within your horse's cells is an ongoing process and is necessary for the production of energy to fuel work, maintenance, and normal metabolic pathways.

As a result of oxidation, free radicals are formed – many thousands of them each day. And they have an important function in destroying bacteria and viruses, serving a role in protecting your horse's immune function. But if the horse is experiencing physical or mental stressors (e.g., strenuous exercise, illness, pain, traveling, stall confinement, etc.), the level of free radical formation can overpower the body's ability to counteract them, leading to the destruction of normal, healthy cells.

A free radical is an unbalanced molecule; it is missing an electron. To ease this "discomfort," the free radical will steal an electron from balanced cells, starting a chain reaction of "electron stealing" from cell to cell, leading to tissue damage, disease, and accelerated aging.

The antioxidant is the hero – it stops this damaging rampage in its tracks by giving of itself – donating its own electron to the free radical. Since the antioxidant is now unstable itself, *it is important to include several antioxidants in the diet to ensure that the unstable one is neutralized and able to function again.*

Principal References

Kutzner-Mulligan, J., Hewitt, K., Sharlette, J., Smith, J., and Pratt-Phillips, S. 2011.The effect of different feed delivery methods on rate of feed consumption and serum insulin concentration in horses. *Journal of Equine Veterinary Science, 31*(5), 300. North Carolina State University.

Moreaux, S.J. J., Nichols, J.L., Bowman, J.G.P., and Hatfield, P.G. 1022. Psyllium lowers blood glucose and insulin concentrations in horses. *Journal of Equine Veterinary Science, 31*, 106-165. Montana State University.

Nielsen, B.D., Vick, M.M., and Dennis, P.M. 2012. A potential link between insulin resistance and iron overload disorder in browsing rhinoceroses investigated through the use of an equine model. *Journal of Zoo and Wildlife Medicine, 43*(3), S61–S65.

Printed in Great Britain
by Amazon.co.uk, Ltd.,
Marston Gate.